Brilliantly Dyslexic

Brilliantly Dyslexic

WRITTEN BY LIZ TRUDEAU

This is a work of creative nonfiction. While the events are substantially true, the depiction is creative and not exhaustive. The stories offer glimpses into the lives of the individuals featured but do not cover all of their accomplishments or struggles.

Disclaimer: Unless otherwise noted, *Brilliantly Dyslexic* is not endorsed by or affiliated with individuals in the book.

The creator is not responsible for websites (or their content) that are not owned by the creator.

Brilliantly Dyslexic is available at special quantity discounts for bulk purchase for sale promotions, fundraising, and educational needs. For details, write to wholesale@brilliantlydyslexic.com. For other inquiries, contact hello@brilliantlydyslexic.com.

Library of Congress Control Number: 2021917754

ISBN 978-1-7377696-1-3 (hardcover)
ISBN 978-1-7377696-0-6 (ebook)

First Edition

Creative Director: Quinn Trudeau
Cover Design: Linda Baritski
Book Design: Kristine Brogno
Editor: S. Robin Larin

Printed in Canada.

TO EVERYONE WHO WONDERS
WHETHER THEY ARE GOOD ENOUGH.

YOU ARE.

CONTENTS

STORIES

Stories

ILLUSTRATION BY
GILLIAN DREHER

Space Scientist

MAGGIE ADERIN-POCOCK

ENGLAND ✶ BORN MARCH 9, 1968

ONCE UPON A TIME in London, England, a little girl dreamed of the stars.

Young Maggie navigated a tumultuous childhood, experiencing her parents' divorce and then going to thirteen different schools before she turned eighteen. She felt like an outsider because she was Black and struggled in school because she was dyslexic.

One ordinary day, Maggie found herself at the library. Rummaging in the nonfiction section, she found a book with an astronaut on the cover. He was floating among the stars with the Earth behind him. *Magical*, thought Maggie. In that moment, in that little London library, she decided she wanted to be an astronaut.

Dreams are tricky, though. Maggie's first obstacle came in elementary school. She felt like school was all about reading and writing, the things that were the most difficult for her. "I just felt incredibly dumb, and all my amazing dreams were coming to nothing. [They were] just crashing to the ground," Maggie says.

One morning, she told a teacher she wanted to be an astronaut. The teacher suggested that she should try something easier instead. Maggie was crushed.

Although many people around her were skeptical, her father was not. Feeding her appetite for information, he took her on long bus trips to and from the library. His support, Maggie says, made it seem "entirely reasonable that with hard work, a Black girl with learning difficulties would soon be traveling from inner London to outer space." He would tell her, "Maggie, you've got challenges, and it might take you longer, but you will get there."

So she kept working. Outside of school, Maggie devoured everything she could find about space—books, cartoons, and television shows.

Then one day, her elementary teacher asked a question in a science lesson. "If one liter of water weighs one kilogram, how much will one cubic centimeter weigh?" *I know this,* Maggie thought, and she raised her hand and got it right. Then she realized that no one else had raised their hand. *Hold it,* she thought. *Maybe I'm not as dumb as I think, and maybe I'm not as dumb as they think. Science gets people to space. If I can do well in science, maybe my dream could come true.*

Maggie continued to lean into her interests. When she was fifteen, she saved up her allowance to buy a telescope. Disappointed with the quality, Maggie enrolled in a build-your-own-telescope class. With the one she created, Maggie could see the rings of Saturn and the moons of Jupiter. Unbeknownst to Maggie, this was the first of many, many instruments she would design.

Some science jobs required a lot of writing. *That's not for me,* Maggie thought. Instead, she chose jobs in the space industry where she could build things. And build things she did. Maggie made enormous telescopes, photographic instruments for space satellites, and systems to help climate research.

Now also a popular TV presenter in Britain, Maggie is passionate about getting people excited about science, especially children. She still dreams of going to space herself . . . perhaps even retiring on Mars. But even more, she wants everyone to know that "you don't need a brain the size of a small planet" to understand and enjoy science.

"We don't encourage kids to aim high in case they fall over. I say—go for it. Failing isn't a problem—interesting things happen along the way, as any entrepreneur will tell you."

DR. MAGGIE ADERIN-POCOCK

ILLUSTRATION BY GERALDINE SY

Polar Explorer

ANN BANCROFT

USA ✶ BORN 1955

EIGHT-YEAR-OLD ANN opened her eyes to the wintry sky. Her half-formed igloo had blocked the wind but not the inch of snow that had fallen overnight. Shaking it off, Ann called to her dog, "Come on, Tommy, time for breakfast!"

Even as a baby, Ann Bancroft was an adventurer. She crawled off on expeditions to the orchard and climbed fearlessly up the family bookshelves.

On those same bookshelves, she later discovered stories about real explorers. Her favorite was about Shackleton's Antarctic expedition. Photographs showed ships trapped in ice, bundled-up figures playing soccer in the snow, and sled dogs in tiny dog igloos. *That's for me*, she thought. "I could see myself in those pictures. The adventure! The dogs!" she recalls.

Soon she was building igloos in her yard, cutting blocks from the deep Minnesota snow. "It was a disaster. I'd get the walls halfway up, and the roof would cave in." Undaunted, she'd turn instead to setting up camp.

She'd gather some blankets, then recruit a cousin to camp out. By morning, however, the shivering cousin was vowing, "Never again!" Soon it was just Ann and Tommy.

Meanwhile, Ann was scraping through school. When she found out in seventh grade that she had dyslexia, "It felt horrible," she remembers. "You just want to be the same as everyone else; you don't want to be different."

Even worse, tutoring pulled her away from the things she loved, like art and sports. Ann hid behind doors and playground equipment to avoid capture, but someone always dragged her back inside to work on her reading.

Nonetheless, Ann decided to become a teacher. "Arctic explorer isn't exactly a career path. I knew teaching was a fit because I had been a coach and camp counselor. I just had to get through school," she says. It wasn't easy, but she graduated and began teaching special education and physical education. She loved being a teacher, and her students loved her.

All along, Ann kept exploring, filling her weekends with outdoor adventures. Then one day, Ann was invited on the trip of her dreams to the North Pole. She hated to leave her students, but she had to go.

She trained for months. Bundled up just like one of Shackleton's crew, she traveled a thousand miles by dogsled to become the first woman to reach the North Pole.

When she returned to her school, she couldn't believe it: "I had disappeared for a year with no way to communicate, and the teachers had brought [my trip] alive through art, songs, poetry, math. They even had pen pals with children in the Arctic."

Ann realized that she could be both a teacher and an explorer! On every trip after that, she planned school lessons and sent updates to all the children following her.

Ann trekked to the South Pole and then faced the greatest challenge of all: skiing across 1,700 miles of snow and ice in Antarctica.

In that frozen wilderness, Ann always felt supported. "Pulling those sleds, I would look back and visualize the kids' faces rooting for me," she says. "They were part of my team."

"I see the goal. I'm not going to get there quickly. I'm not going to get there on anyone else's path. I'm going to get lost some of the time. But I will get there."

ANN BANCROFT

ILLUSTRATION BY PAUL TRUDEAU

Boxer

RUQSANA BEGUM

ENGLAND ✶ BORN 1983

"RUQSANA!" A BOY SHOUTED. "We pick Ruqsana!" The class gathered in the London schoolyard, picking teams for a soccer game. Quick and strong, Ruqsana felt proud to join the boys' team. She sprinted down the field, powerful, unstoppable, her long dress and headscarf rippling in the breeze.

But by the time she was ten, Ruqsana wasn't allowed to play with the boys. "It's unladylike," her mother explained, "and I need you at home."

Growing up in a traditional Bangladeshi family, Ruqsana Begum was expected to be a good Muslim girl: modest, obedient, and able to cook and care for her future husband. Sports and other pursuits weren't on the list.

Ruqsana loved school, but words and numbers would get jumbled up. "I knew I wasn't dumb, but the teachers kept putting me in the lower group," she remembers. "I thought, *'They don't think you can do it. No one believes in you.'*"

Ruqsana worked hard to prove her teachers wrong. Eventually, her high school art teacher suggested she get tested. Ruqsana was relieved to find out she was dyslexic. Her struggles finally made sense, and school became a little easier once she had the right support.

When Ruqsana was seventeen, she noticed a school flyer: "Try Thai Kickboxing! Thursday at 4:00 p.m. in the gym." She had been fascinated by martial arts since she was a little girl watching Bruce Lee on TV. *I have to do this,* Ruqsana thought.

Thursday arrived. Ruqsana waited nervously for the class to begin. Her doubts disappeared the moment she landed her first punch. *Thwack!* She remembered how she felt in the schoolyard all those years ago—powerful.

The coach was so impressed that he invited her to train at his gym for free. She went every Sunday. Soon she was fighting in small matches—and winning! There was only one problem: Her parents would never approve. Knowing this, Ruqsana kept her training a secret. She hid trophies in the back of her closet and bruises under long shirts and pants.

Ruqsana couldn't live a double life forever. After graduating from university, she gave up boxing. She put all her effort into being the good Muslim woman who would make her parents proud. But she was miserable and fell ill. For months, she lay in bed, weak and depressed.

Desperate for change, Ruqsana recalled the energy and strength she felt at the kickboxing gym. She needed to go back. She plucked up her courage and told her parents everything. Concerned for their daughter's health, her parents gave their blessing.

Ruqsana threw herself into training. After only a few matches, she found herself in the World Kickboxing Championship. To everyone's surprise, she won a bronze medal! *Wow, there were 150 countries competing!* she thought. *Imagine if I really dedicated myself.*

A year later, Ruqsana won the British Championship and then the European Championship. She set her sights on the World Championship title. After three attempts, she finally won! She became the first British Muslim female to win a world championship in any sport.

From her early struggles in school to challenging cultural expectations, Ruqsana has learned to take risks and believe in herself.

“Knock me down, but I rise back up.”

RUQSANA BEGUM

ILLUSTRATION BY
GILLIAN DREHER

Doctor
BERYL BENACERRAF

FRANCE + USA ✶ BORN 1949

EVEN AS A LITTLE GIRL, Beryl dreamed of being a doctor. She longed to follow in the footsteps of her father and her uncle who had both won the Nobel Prize in medicine. Science seemed to be in her blood. But she still wondered, *Am I good enough?*

Beryl moved to New York City from France at age eight. When she struggled to read, her teachers thought she was confused by learning two languages. No one knew Beryl had dyslexia.

Despite being a quick thinker, Beryl couldn't read information fast enough for her brain to make sense of it. It was like trying to do a puzzle with the pieces scattered across the room. She wanted to take in the whole page at once, not pick up fragments of ideas word by word. "It was incredibly frustrating. To think quickly but read and write slowly," she says.

Beryl worked hard to hide her difficulties and blend in. She inched along until receiving a D on her report card in seventh-grade English. "Unacceptable," her father said. "I know you're not stupid, because you're my daughter, so you must be lazy. You will do better."

However, between piano lessons, dance lessons, and various other activities her parents insisted on, Beryl didn't have much spare time. She began to beg for assignments in advance so she'd have enough time to complete them. She looked for shortcuts, like watching the movie version of the books she was supposed to read, and she worked extra, extra hard.

College was a little easier. Beryl chose science and math courses, where she excelled. And she found more shortcuts, like paying other students to type and edit her papers.

But when she applied to medical school, Beryl couldn't get in on test scores alone. Her father made phone calls and asked for favors. "I would never have gotten into medical school without him. Kids like me need someone who can open doors for us," she says.

While at Harvard Medical School, Beryl figured out she had dyslexia and that it came with some extraordinary abilities. For example, when she was doing a rotation in radiology, Beryl could find things in X-rays that other people could not. The first time it happened, Beryl thought it was beginner's luck, but it happened again and again. A senior doctor pulled her aside. "In thirty years as a radiologist, I have never seen anyone with talent like yours," he said.

Since others couldn't see what she did, doctors and experts didn't immediately accept Beryl's findings. She was booed off the stage when presenting her conclusions at a conference and denied admittance to medical groups. She learned to persevere and trust herself, believing people would eventually come around.

And they did! Dr. Beryl became a leader in reading ultrasounds of babies in the womb, finding problems sometimes treatable before birth. Today, she is known all over the world for her skills as a radiologist and is a professor at Harvard Medical School.

"Anomalies jump out at me like a neon sign," Beryl says. "I live in a world of patterns and images, and I see things that no one else sees." The unusual way her brain processes information has enabled her to help those in the greatest need.

"If you give someone like me a chance, once I get there, I can prove myself."

BERYL BENACERRAF

ILLUSTRATION BY GERALDINE SY

Entrepreneur

RICHARD BRANSON

ENGLAND ✶ BORN JULY 18, 1950

RICHARD BRANSON'S mother was a force to be reckoned with.

Full of energy and adventure, Eve Branson concocted extraordinary challenges to teach her shy son self-reliance and courage. When Richard was five, she dropped him off a few miles from home and let him find his own way back. When he was eleven, she popped him onto his bicycle with a few sandwiches and an "off you go," sending him to visit family in a town fifty miles away. Richard returned that evening tired but proud.

Although these adventures were terrifying at first, Richard learned to trust himself and face challenges head on. The worst that could happen was that he would fail. And Richard would be no stranger to failure.

When he was eleven, Richard and his friend Nik started a bunny business. They would breed rabbits and sell them. Nik had run the numbers—they were going to be rich! That is, until some rats got in and ate the rabbits. Undeterred, the friends started a Christmas tree business, using their pocket money to plant 1,000 tiny trees. This time, the rabbits got in and ate all the trees.

While these fledgling business flops were disappointing, Richard's challenges in school were the most disheartening. To Richard, words just looked like a jumble on the chalkboard. He was dyslexic but didn't know it. In fact, nobody around him had heard of the word *dyslexia.* "People just thought I was stupid," he recalls. Fortunately, his family made sure he knew this wasn't true, regardless of his report cards. He relied on playing sports to keep his spirits up as he muddled through.

Adventurous, kind, and full of ideas, Richard was a friend magnet. When at fifteen he and his friends were frustrated by their school's many rules and requirements, Richard had an idea: He'd start a student magazine. In it, they could publish their revolutionary thoughts.

They named it *Student* and got to work recruiting contributors and advertisers. Excited about his new venture, Richard began devoting all his spare time to the magazine, dropping most of his classes. He left school at sixteen to work on *Student* full time. His headmaster's parting words were "Congratulations, Branson. I predict you will either go to prison or become a millionaire."

The magazine was just the beginning. When it struggled, Richard started a mail order record business to fund it. A recording studio and record label followed. Richard kept going, building the Virgin Group into over sixty companies. Each new business began with an idea to make something simpler and more fun for people—from mobile phones to air travel—and inviting the smartest people he knew to help make it happen.

Like his childhood bunny business, many of Richard's ideas didn't work out. But he learned to see failure as part of pursuing anything worthwhile. He's now setting his sights on other planets with Virgin Galactic, his space tourism endeavor.

When Richard found out about dyslexia in his mid-twenties, he felt relieved to have an explanation for his challenges in school. Over time, he came to credit dyslexia for his greatest talents: creativity, unconventional thinking, and a "knack for bringing together wonderful people" to create amazing things. Playing to these strengths, Richard learned to reach for the stars.

"It is only through failure that we learn. Many of the world's finest minds have learned this the hard way."

RICHARD BRANSON

ILLUSTRATION BY MONICA GARWOOD

Dancer

DARCEY BUSSELL

ENGLAND ✶ BORN APRIL 27, 1969

AS A SMALL CHILD, Darcey Bussell was a master of escape. At school, when it was time for the subjects that she found difficult—like reading, writing, and math—Darcey would mysteriously disappear. Her teacher would later find her nestled in a closet among the workbooks and pencils. When she couldn't pull her disappearing act, she'd find other ways to "escape" tasks that felt impossible. If Darcey had an hour in class to write an illustrated story, she'd spend almost all her time drawing, "accidentally" running out of time to write the story.

Darcey was eleven when she discovered that she was dyslexic. At first, she felt discouraged. *I was sort of hoping this would just magically go away,* she thought. With the diagnosis, however, Darcey was better understood by her teachers and could get better support. Over time, she created little tricks that helped at school. For example, instead of writing and reviewing study notes, she would record herself speaking about a subject and then listen to the playback.

With strategies to help, Darcey stopped hiding from schoolwork and took it on as a challenge. She recalls, "I would never give in. I was also clear that life isn't all about academic grades. I still had ways of doing well." Two areas in which Darcey excelled were art and sports. She loved drawing, doing gymnastics, and even playing on the boys' soccer team.

But it was dance that had been Darcey's passion since she was a small child. It gave her an outlet for the emotions that didn't come out easily in words. Even so, Darcey had never thought about dancing as a possible career—until one day, when a teacher told her that she had the right physique to be a decent dancer. She set her mind to becoming a ballerina.

At age thirteen, Darcey passed the audition to get into Britain's Royal Ballet School. But at this elite level, her skills were far behind her classmates' abilities. During Darcey's first year, the older girls laughed at her as she tried to copy their steps. Her exams were so disastrous that she burst into tears. But she kept working.

A year later, something remarkable happened: Darcey suddenly improved. All her previous hard work started showing up in the form of exceptional technique. At sixteen, Darcey progressed to the next level of the Royal Ballet School, and at eighteen, she joined the Sadler's Wells Royal Ballet, a professional dance company. Just two years later, Darcey returned to the Royal Ballet, but not as a student. Now she was a principal dancer.

Darcey danced as the principal ballerina for the Royal Ballet for twenty years. She was known for her unique combination of athleticism, emotion, and grace. Over her career, she performed more than eighty roles, including Aurora in four different productions of *Sleeping Beauty*.

Darcey came a long way from the little girl with dyslexia hiding in the closet. With a lot of determination, she learned "to always work difficulties into my favor and find a way around them."

“Work hard, be focused, appreciate your strengths, and you can always, always prove people wrong.”

DARCEY BUSSELL

ILLUSTRATION BY ANNIE GALVIN

Artist

HEATHER DAY

USA ✶ BORN JANUARY 31, 1989

TURN, STRAIGHT, CURVE, STOP. Heather sat in the back seat of the family car, her sketchbook in hand. As they drove, she followed the movement with her pencil. When the car turned, so did her line. By the time her family arrived at their destination, Heather had a map—not one that you could follow to get from point A to B, but one that expressed her experience of traveling.

As early as she can remember, art was Heather's home. Art opened doors to a world of exploration, where she could turn old cereal boxes into robots and use paints and pastels to create feeling and movement on blank paper.

School, in contrast, felt like a foreign land, one built with words, straight lines, and right answers. It felt rigid and constraining. "I've always been a bit lost in this concrete, logical, wordy world," she says.

Although she didn't know it until fifth grade, Heather was dyslexic. Learning through language was a challenge; she felt more comfortable when ideas were expressed in more than one way. She needed more time to unpack her thoughts into words.

She hated being one of the kids in the class who struggled. It was embarrassing. Yet Heather persevered, often feeling she had to work five times harder than her classmates. Pushing through the embarrassment, she learned to speak up when she didn't understand and spent time with teachers, getting extra help.

All the while, her parents encouraged her as she dove into art—a place where she felt free and confident.

In 2008, Heather began studying at the Maryland Institute College of Art. After graduating, she moved to San Francisco. There, she woke up at 5:00 a.m. every morning to work in her studio before going to her job selling furniture at the San Francisco Design Center, only to return home and paint until midnight.

And then Heather took a big risk. She quit her job to pursue painting full time. As she jumped into her practice, Heather looked back on the times she viewed her dyslexia as a disability. She thought, *I might have been looking at it all wrong. Dyslexia may have made it difficult to grasp the language of words. But it also enhanced my experience of the world of color and painting.*

In Heather's art, there are no right answers. She invites people into an experience of free-form expression. It's a place without words, rules, and concrete forms, like trees, people, and buildings. Instead, she works with colors, emotion, and movement—the things that can be felt but not held.

Heather thinks of each painting as a rough draft that leads to her next piece. "My work is largely unplanned, and I rely on the element of the accident paired with intention," she says.

Heather's work has been shown around the world, from New York to Seoul, and is held in countless collections. But being a professional artist isn't just about creating art; it involves contracts with galleries, collaborating with company brands, and carrying out campaigns. So that she can focus on creating, Heather has a whole team to help—from a studio manager to various gallerists. Heather learned that she doesn't have to do it all herself. She just needs to be her best self.

“No matter who you are or what you’re grappling with, and no matter your level, art will meet you where you are and take you somewhere good.”

HEATHER DAY

ILLUSTRATION BY MERCEDES DEBELLARD

Behavioral Ecologist

KATE EVANS

ENGLAND ✶ BORN 1975

"WHERE'S ITS MOTHER?" Kate asked, gazing at the baby elephant. "It looks lost and sad." Seven-year-old Kate was visiting an elephant sanctuary in Sri Lanka when a young elephant arrived alone. She and her family were on a trip from Pakistan where her father was in the British foreign service.

The little elephant looked terrified, and Kate was heartbroken. *This poor, beautiful creature is so scared and so confused and must be wondering where its family is,* Kate thought. She made a vow to the elephant: *I'm going to do something to make this better. I promise.*

Kate held on to that promise as she went off to boarding school in England. Plastering her walls with pictures of elephants and declaring her dream to save them, she quickly became known as "Elephant Kate," a nickname she carried with pride.

She was known for other things too, like sports, but never for good grades. "I would get things wrong, but I didn't understand why, especially in English," Kate says.

Luckily, she had Mr. Joseph, her ancient history teacher. "He would teach us little sayings, like 'G-A-S . . . everyone is Good At Something.'" His encouragement kept Kate going even as she struggled.

Despite her grades, Kate squeaked through university admissions and went on to study zoology. Able to focus on her passion, she did quite well in her classes. After graduation, she set off for Africa. For her PhD, Kate designed a project studying elephants released into the wild. Living in a tent at the edge of a national park in northern Botswana, she followed the elephants every day. She was alone on expansive flood plains with the elephants, leopards, lions, and antelope. "It was just me and a 4x4," Kate recalls. She loved it.

When Kate returned to England to complete her PhD, she felt as though she were back in grade school. Everything seemed to be going wrong, and she didn't understand why. One day she took a dyslexia test. At twenty-nine, she heard, "Kate, you're dyslexic. You have a reading age of twelve."

Her confidence plummeted. *I'm not good enough. I might as well give up now,* she thought. But her friends and family would have none of that. They told her, "*You've* achieved this PhD. *You've* gotten there. This has been all *you.* Does it really matter that you're not spectacular at reading and writing?"

Kate decided to believe them and refocus on her promise. *I'm not giving up,* she thought. *I'm going to get through it.*

And she did.

Dr. Kate went back to Botswana and started Elephants for Africa. She and her team study elephants, asking questions like, *Why do elephants like one friend over another? Why do they like going to this part of the river but not that part? What makes them feel happy and safe?*

They use what they learn to help people and elephants live together without hurting each other. For example, "If we know that elephants hate the sound of bees and hate the smell of chili peppers, how can we use that information to keep the elephants out of the villages and the crops?"

It's challenging work with slow results, but she's committed. "I'm doing what I set out to do. I've gotten to follow through on my promise."

“I’ve never taken the common path. I’ve always taken my own.”

KATE EVANS

ILLUSTRATION BY CHRIS KING

Hair Stylist
VERNON FRANÇOIS

ENGLAND ✶ BORN 1985

"OW!" VERNON EXCLAIMED, his head jerking to the side. It was Sunday afternoon. This meant two things in the François household: chicken and rice stewing on the stove and all the children getting their hair done in braids, locs, and twists. The results were often beautiful, but the process was painful.

After his turn, Vernon wasn't happy with what he saw in the mirror. "If you don't like it, do it yourself!" his mother snapped. *Fine!* Vernon thought. *I'm gonna show you that I can braid better than you.* Vernon was eight, and it was the last time his mother did his hair.

Vernon got to work experimenting, starting with the rugs in the house. He'd turn the fringe along the edge into a multitude of neat braids down one side and one long twist down the other. He'd unravel each rope of the kitchen mop head and spend hours creating box braids, cornrows, and fishtails. Anything in the house that could be braided would be braided.

Eventually, Vernon got his hands on a doll's head. She had big blue eyes and long, silky blond hair. He named her Shaniqua, and she lived hidden away under his bed when he wasn't practicing his styling skills on her.

While Vernon was becoming a master with hair, he was floundering in school. His classmates mocked him for not being able to read or spell things correctly. Rather than spotting his dyslexia, his teachers dismissed him as having no potential and a bad attitude. "School was a very, very, very dark space," Vernon says. He felt stupid and misunderstood.

Every day after school, he'd race home to Shaniqua. Alone in his room, braiding and re-braiding her hair, he felt confident and capable.

When he was fourteen, Vernon's family moved to London. He got a job at Burlington's, a fancy salon in Oxford Circus. While he cleaned the windows and swept the floor, he studied the stylists' techniques and peppered them with questions about cutting, blow-drying, and makeup.

Like other top salons, Burlington's focused on straight and wavy hair. They didn't know what to do when someone with highly textured hair showed up, so they'd turn them away. One day, when a curly-haired client arrived, Vernon piped up, "I can do it." Surrounded by beautiful, coily hair his whole life, he knew exactly what to do.

From then on, the salon stopped sending curls away and started sending them to Vernon. Soon he was working full time as a stylist.

At sixteen, Vernon won Newcomer of the Year at the Black Beauty Hair Awards. Word got out, and he became the go-to guy for curls and coils. Black musicians touring Europe called him in to do their hair. Impressed by his creativity and skill, stars like Lupita Nyong'o started asking Vernon to style their hair for television shows, movies, and ultimately the Oscars.

Today, while many hair stylists try to minimize frizz and tame curls, Vernon unleashes them. He celebrates being creative with kinks, curls, and frizz, working with them for shape and volume. He teaches his clients, "Your hair has its own personality. You have to learn to love it. What does my hair love to do? How can I amplify that? Your hair is beautiful the way it is."

Likewise, Vernon learned to embrace his dyslexia as part of what has made him wildly creative, beautiful, and strong.

"It's about loving what you already have, learning to see and embrace your own beauty."

VERNON FRANÇOIS

ILLUSTRATION BY HSIAO-RON CHENG

Designer
JOHN HOKE

USA ✶ BORN 1964

JOHN LOVED SHOES. He was fascinated with how they looked, how they worked, and how they were made. One summer afternoon, as John floated in a public pool, his mind drifted yet again to shoes. *What if I could shrink this inflatable raft and wrap it around my foot?* he thought. *What would it be like to run in that?*

That night, with his dad's help, John sketched a blueprint for the raft shoe. He decided to share his idea with his favorite shoe company. Nike wrote back, "Thanks! Here's a free pair of shoes and a T-shirt. When you're older, come work for us."

Growing up, John was always doodling—even during class. It was his way of thinking things through. But while drawing came naturally, reading and writing were chores. John found reading exhausting, and his letters were either backward or upside down. *What is wrong with me?* he wondered. *Everybody else seems to do this easily.*

In second grade, John found out he had dyslexia and got tutoring to help. To get his letters going in the right direction, he spent hours practicing. He drew the alphabet over and over again, focusing on how each letter looked and precisely how the lines came together. To John's surprise, not only did his writing improve, but his drawing did too.

John doubled down on practicing, sketching for hours, drawing and redrawing. As a result, he became a masterful artist.

John's parents encouraged his creativity and helped him work around the things that tripped him up. "You know, John, you just see the world differently," his mother said. "You have a different path." When John came home from school with thick textbooks, she would read them aloud to him. John's teachers made space for him as well. They accepted his untraditional reports that combined words—sometimes misspelled, upside down, or backward—with drawings.

When it came time for college, though, John wasn't quite sure what to do. "I knew I was smart. I knew I could hustle like anyone," he says. "But I didn't have the test scores." He had, however, developed his other talents. In 1984, he became one of a handful of students accepted on artistic merit into the architecture program at Penn State.

After college, John worked as an architect before returning to graduate school in 1991. There, John began thinking about Nike again. He contacted the design department, and they invited him to interview for a job. John shared a portfolio of his best work, saving a little surprise for the end. He slid Nike's long-ago response to his raft-shoe design across the table and announced, "I'm here to redeem this coupon."

John got the job and worked his way up to Chief Design Officer. He and his team design Nike's shoes, clothing, and more. They explore big questions like, *How can we help all athletes fulfill their potential? What records and barriers in sport remain unbroken? How might we make our products as planet friendly as possible? Could clothing ever feel like it's part of your body? What about a shoe that feels like walking on grass . . . or floating on a raft?*

Whatever the challenge, for John, it always starts with drawing. "I'm drawing all the time," John says. "It's how I think."

"My first real language was drawing."

JOHN HOKE

ILLUSTRATION BY LI ZHANG

Venture Capitalist

DAVID HORNIK

USA ✶ BORN 1968

"PASS THE PEAS, and Dad, you've got to be kidding." Young David shook his head. "School uniforms?"

Mr. Hornik had kicked off the nightly dinnertime debate with the school board's idea of a new dress code. "It'll be less distracting," he explained. The table exploded in a flurry of objections, each Hornik making their case.

David was in the center of it all, voicing his opinions loudly and keeping the family laughing. His quick thinking and wit regularly challenged and entertained his family.

So when teachers invited only his older sister and younger brother to the gifted program, his mother was baffled. "What about David?" Betsy Hornik inquired. "I assure you, David is as smart as the others."

Testing confirmed Betsy's opinion: David's low reading and writing scores sat next to very high scores in areas like problem solving. "See. I told you he was smart," she summarized. To David, she made her opinion clear: "You're doing well in the things that really matter. These other things, we can work on them. But someone can check your spelling!"

Still, at school, the message was clear: Readers are smart. Smart kids read. David wondered, *What about the smart kids who don't read?*

While his classmates relied on textbooks, David listened carefully in class, figuring out what really mattered about the subject. He talked his way into alternative assignments. "Rather than that five-page paper, how 'bout I write you a play? Or give a speech?"

Betsy Hornik was always there for support. They wrote papers together, David speaking while she typed and critiqued. "She would never allow sloppy work," David says. Knowing David learned best by listening, she read aloud. What mattered was learning, not how he did it.

Outside the classroom, David threw himself into the things he loved: music, singing, and acting. He shone on stage and loved being the center of attention. By the time David graduated in 1986, he was one of the best violinists in New Hampshire. He imagined a future playing in an orchestra.

However, in college, David set his sights on becoming a lawyer. "The idea of being in a courtroom and arguing for a living seemed like a no-brainer," he says. He carved a path through college, finding classes that played to his interests, like music and technology, and rewarded him for good arguments, like political science.

Law school was brutal. There was no way around the reading, but David worked extra hard. He survived and became a lawyer.

Then in 2000, a well-known venture capitalist noticed at several meetings how David saw the "big picture" and was good with people. "Have you ever thought about the venture business?" he asked.

Betting on people with ideas to solve big problems, even the best venture capitalists are wrong more often than right. But it was a perfect fit for David. He would be talking to people about ideas, chatting with experts about technology, and sharing his opinions about what to do next.

David has become one of Silicon Valley's top venture capitalists, investing in dozens of tech companies and helping them succeed and grow.

And his mother's response when David told her about his new career? "You've talked your way into a job that only involves talking," Betsy Hornik replied. "Perfect."

“Just because I misspell it doesn’t mean it isn’t true.”

DAVID HORNIK

ILLUSTRATION BY LIAM BRAZIER

Basketball Player

EARVIN "MAGIC" JOHNSON

USA ✶ BORN 1959

THUNK, THUNK, THUNK. Little Earvin's family could always hear him coming. From the moment his father gave him a basketball in elementary school, it was his constant companion. He dribbled it everywhere, day and night. It annoyed the neighbors to no end. Little did they know that this boy would become one of the best basketball players the world had ever seen.

Earvin and his nine brothers and sisters grew up in Lansing, Michigan. His mother was a school custodian. His father worked at an auto factory during the day and hauled trash at night, often bringing Earvin along to help. Earvin's father didn't accept any slacking off. "My parents believed in work—not only for themselves but their children too," Earvin recalls. That included chores at home. Earvin's basketball career began with rolling his freshly washed socks into balls and using the laundry basket as his hoop.

Once school and chores were done and he made it out onto the court, Earvin never wanted to leave. Even dinner couldn't lure him away; his mom would hide his plate from his siblings so he could eat when he came home.

With no money for fancy basketball shoes, Earvin played in $1.99 sneakers from Walgreens. When the soles wore away, he would keep on playing, owning the court with holes in his shoes. "As hard as my father worked on his jobs," Earvin says, "I worked on the basketball court."

Five blocks from Earvin's house was Sexton High, a basketball powerhouse. Earvin had grown up watching the team play and couldn't wait for his turn on the court. But when he reached high school, he was bussed across the city to Everett High, whose basketball team was ranked dead last.

Earvin was devastated, but he doubled down on his training and devoted himself to improving the team. Soon, with Earvin's skill and enthusiasm, they weren't just winning, they were dominating. After a spectacular win against the number one team, a newspaper reporter dubbed him "Magic." Earvin was only fifteen, but the name stuck.

Earvin was magic on the court but floundering in the classroom. If he wanted to go to college, he needed to attend summer school. He hated the idea, but he was barely passing, and his classmates made fun of him when he read aloud. So Earvin worked as hard on his reading as he did on the court, and his grades improved.

When Michigan State offered him a scholarship, Magic became the first person in his family to go to college. He led his team to win the National College Championship. Shortly after, the Lakers chose him as their number one draft pick. He cried when they handed him his NBA jersey, realizing he could finally give something back to his parents. He bought them a house and sent them on their first real vacation.

With the Lakers, Magic won five championships, handfuls of MVP awards, and an Olympic gold medal. After retiring from basketball, Earvin didn't slow down. He shifted his focus to giving back. He invests in low-income communities, offers education scholarships, and visits schools around the country, telling his story and encouraging students to work hard for their dreams. "I got my mother's smile," he says, "and her desire to give back to the world."

“If you don’t dream it, you can’t become it.”

EARVIN “MAGIC” JOHNSON

ILLUSTRATION BY
JUSTINE LECOUFFE

Politician & Diplomat

CAROL MOSELEY BRAUN

USA ✶ BORN 1947

"DUCK AND COVER!" Carol's teacher yelled.

The third-grade students at Martha M. Ruggles Elementary School scrambled under their desks. Carol crouched in the back row as people hurled stones and insults from the street. She knew they were meant for her. Carol was one of the first Black students in a previously all-white school.

Angry parents weren't her only problem. Carol learned differently. Her brain turned letters around and filled in the wrong endings to words. Her new teacher promptly put her in the "dummy row." Carol was outraged. *But I love to learn, and I'm smart,* she thought. *I will not be counted out.*

Determined to prove herself, Carol worked extra hard. She spent hours using a ruler to calm the letters on the page, improving her reading enough to get by. She showed her intelligence when answering her teachers' questions out loud. They soon realized they had misjudged her and changed how they treated her. Carol had fought back and won.

Carol grew up amid the civil rights movement, the fight to change laws discriminating against people because of their skin color. Black people were told where to live, go to school, work, and eat. Carol's father, a police officer and activist, taught her that if you want something to change, you have to fight to change it. Her mother encouraged her, "Grow where you are planted. Do the best job you can at whatever you are doing."

When her parents divorced, teenaged Carol, her siblings, and her mother moved in with her grandmother. Carol went from a peaceful suburb to a poor, overcrowded neighborhood so violent people called it the "bucket of blood." It was "like moving to a different planet," she remembers.

Until then, Carol hadn't known about the deep poverty of "fifteen people in a one-bedroom apartment, with roaches crawling on the walls." She was heartbroken and appalled by what she saw.

After college, Carol became a lawyer, seeing it as the best way to make a difference and a living. When asked to run for Illinois state government, she dismissed the idea. Then one man told her, "Don't run. You can't possibly win. The whites won't vote for you, because you're Black, and nobody is going to vote for you, because you are a woman." *That needs to change,* Carol thought. *Count me in.*

In 1978, surprising everyone—including herself—she won!

Carol worked hard as a legislator. She had a talent for pulling people together from different backgrounds and beliefs to agree on big things like education, poverty, and equal rights.

When Carol didn't like what she saw in Washington DC, she decided to run for the US Senate. She had the right experience but the wrong image. People expected a senator to be a gray-haired white man. Newspapers asked, "Is it possible? A Black woman elected to the US Senate?" Up against a popular senator and a millionaire, Carol would surely lose the race.

Against the odds, she won! In 1993, Carol became the first Black woman to serve in the history of the US Senate. She has also been US ambassador to New Zealand and Samoa, carrying her message of equality around the world. The little girl who was counted out in third grade made sure her life would count for others.

“It wasn’t about winning or losing. I was just trying to do the right thing.”

CAROL MOSELEY BRAUN

ILLUSTRATION BY DÉBORA ISLAS

Software Engineer
MARIA NAGGAGA

UGANDA ✶ BORN 1983

THE FIRST TIME THEY MET, Maria felt an instant spark. Her new friend was different, a behind-the-scenes type, and Maria was enamored. They met by chance in Maria's favorite café, and she would never forget that moment—the moment she saw computer code for the first time.

Maria was eighteen, living in Kampala, Uganda. While browsing the internet, she accidentally clicked the wrong button. A window popped open, revealing the code for the web page. Stunned, she thought, *This is the easiest thing I've read in my life.*

Eager to learn more, she downloaded her discovery onto a flash drive and dashed home. She started editing the files, somehow instinctively knowing what to do. When she finished, Maria sat back. On screen was her first creation, a fan page for the pop group Destiny's Child.

School didn't come easily for Maria. At the time, few people in Uganda knew about dyslexia or how to help. Maria's teachers divided the class into "group A: the smart kids, group B: ok, group C: all the children they forgot about," Maria recalls. They gave Maria's group C simple tasks and sometimes wouldn't even show up to teach them. Overlooked and unseen, Maria had the lowest grades in her class from age seven to sixteen. *When will I get past this?* she wondered.

Doing well in school meant everything in Uganda, and Maria felt worthless. Maria's parents saw her differently. "What the school says doesn't matter. There are other ways you are smart," they said. "Your journey is different." Her father sat for hours reading history books to her, filling her hungry mind with all the things she couldn't read and the school wasn't teaching her.

Once Maria connected with coding, they became inseparable. She created a website to showcase her art, fan pages for artists she loved, and even a maze game she called *Pies and Robots.* She felt empowered. Finally, she had something she was proud of.

Maria's mother encouraged her to take some computer science classes. Maria excelled. She came away with grades that would get her into university and the confidence she could succeed. In 2007, she set off for school in Canada.

One day, a professor told Maria, "I think you're dyslexic." Sheepishly, Maria responded, "Oh, yeah, I am. It's a bit embarrassing." "Why?" he asked. "I'm dyslexic. Several other professors are too, and there is a center here on campus that can help."

For the rest of university, Maria had a coach. They worked on tricks, like different ways to take notes in class. She got extra time on exams, but by her final year, she didn't need it anymore. Maria learned to play to her strengths and saw that her dyslexia wasn't a weakness; her journey was merely different.

After college, Maria joined a large computer company. There, she developed video games and computer programs and finally began working with computer coding language itself—her first love.

Now every day she asks, *How do we make code simpler, faster, and stronger for the millions of people creating with it? When a child meets code for the first time, how can we make it love at first sight?* Using technology, Maria continues to work on making the world a more inclusive place for everyone, including people just like her.

"Being able to do this one thing well gave me the confidence to do other things well."

MARIA NAGGAGA

ILLUSTRATION BY MARTA SIGNORI

Journalist

BYRON PITTS

USA ✶ BORN 1960

BYRON WAS A BOY WITH SECRETS. Only his family and a few friends knew he stuttered. But the real secret, the one nobody knew, was that he couldn't read.

Byron grew up in East Baltimore, Maryland. His mother, Clarise, worked two jobs, raising three kids and attending night school. She assumed that Byron had learned to read along with his classmates.

As time passed, Byron began to wonder, *How long can I keep this up?* In fifth grade, his Ds dropped to Fs, and a note came home: "Byron is failing math." After some testing, his secret was out. "It wasn't that I couldn't do the math; I could not read the directions," he says.

Clarise Pitts ran on hope the way cars run on gas. "If you work hard and pray hard and treat people right, good things will happen," she told her son.

With little support coming from school, Clarise Pitts convinced an adult reading program to help. A machine that looked like a TV arrived at the Pitts' door. Every day, Byron spent an hour with the reading machine. The first lesson was on the alphabet. Byron was eleven and learning to recognize and sound out letters for the first time.

As if scaling a mountain, he slowly made progress, step by step. Still, he worried—would he ever catch up to his classmates? Clarise Pitts, however, was confident: "Son, it doesn't matter how you start, only how you finish."

With the help of his mother, his coaches, and his teachers, Byron stayed focused and kept working. He would learn to read. He would go to college. He would make his mother proud. By the time he graduated high school, he had worked his way up from the bottom of his class to near the top.

Still, college was difficult. The work was harder, the deadlines tighter, and the expectations higher. Byron almost gave up in the beginning. Yet he wasn't alone: His mother's weekly letters encouraged him to persevere.

Byron wanted to be a journalist. A job full of reading and speaking? It was a surprising choice for a boy who couldn't read until he was twelve or speak clearly until he was twenty.

However, through all those years wrestling with words, Byron wasn't merely conquering them, he was falling in love with them. "I love words more than the average person because when you haven't had something, you appreciate it more," he says.

Every night he announced the news into his bathroom mirror with a toothbrush microphone. "I'm Byron Pitts. Here's today's news . . ." When the time came, he would be prepared.

Graduating from college and his bathroom mirror broadcasts, Byron got a job as a journalist. He started at the bottom, taking jobs all around the country. Finally, he landed his dream job at CBS, later becoming an anchor on *Nightline* at ABC. He has interviewed presidents and world leaders and covered the biggest news stories of his time.

Along the way, Byron learned that every good story is about struggle—between dreams and disappointment, love and loss, life and death. Because of his own battles, he has a unique talent for bringing these stories to life. Rather than defeating him, Byron's own struggles have fueled his success.

"Hard work never lies."

BYRON PITTS

ILLUSTRATION BY MONICA GARWOOD

Pastry Chef

ELISABETH PRUEITT

USA ✶ BORN 1963

MEASURING, MELTING, AND MIXING, Liz danced around the kitchen. The scents of chocolate and vanilla seeped under her apartment door and drifted down the hallway. The neighbors sniffed hopefully. Liz was baking again!

Liz grew up in a family of makers. Her father was an artist and writer, and her mother was a graphic designer, sewer, and knitter. If they weren't playing in Prospect Park or exploring the local museum in her hometown of Brooklyn, New York, they were creating a dessert for a dinner party, a dollhouse with tiny furniture, or a drawing of imaginary creatures.

This life was perfect for Liz, who loved working with her hands.

When she started school, however, Liz quickly felt stuck. Letters looked confusing, and she wrote in reverse. With the help of a reading specialist, Liz was soon reading well.

But expressing ideas on paper still felt impossible. Complicated instructions paralyzed her, and math became her worst enemy. "It felt like sand slipping through my fingers," Liz says. In class, Liz tried to make herself invisible, silently pleading, *Please don't call on me. Please don't call on me.*

Liz felt wired to see, experience, and express things differently. *Everyone else has this knowledge that I don't have,* she thought. *There must be a guidebook I'm missing.* She was drenched in an "overwhelming feeling of frustration."

The kitchen, in contrast, felt like freedom. Liz spent long afternoons exploring different textures, tastes, and ingredients. Baking helped her master multistep instructions, and she flew through the *Joy of Cooking*, whipping up cookies and cakes. The recipes became like good friends, reliable and forgiving. She trusted them, and if she messed something up, she could always try again.

After high school and a brief stint in college, Liz began waitressing to earn a living. But she was always baking—for her roommates, friends, and family. One friend finally urged her, "Go to culinary school. This is what you are good at."

Culinary school was heaven. "I was getting straight As and loving every minute of it," Liz recalls, even with papers to write and math and chemistry to master. Every day she practiced techniques and recipes—croissants, cakes, and custards—over and over again. After years of comparing herself to others, she realized she had different talents. "My mind, my hands, they were made to make things. This is what I was born to do," she says.

In 1995, Liz settled in Point Reyes, a sleepy village north of San Francisco, and got to the business of baking. She happily concocted tray upon tray of perfect pastries in the wood-fired oven of her little farmhouse.

Word got around about Liz's creations. One day, a famous California chef arrived at her garden gate: Alice Waters. Impressed, she bought piles of pastries and left Liz bursting with pride.

In 2002, Liz and her partner opened Tartine Bakery in San Francisco to the delight of customers who gladly wait in long lines for her delicious desserts. More bakeries and restaurants have followed. Liz's cookbooks, full of perfected classics and original creations, are used by chefs and bakers around the world. "I'm always trying to make it better than the last time," she says. Ever exploring in the kitchen, Liz has baked her way from frustration to acclaim.

“I can best express myself—and am happiest—using my brain and hands and eyes to bake and make art.”

ELISABETH PRUEITT

ILLUSTRATION BY JUSTINE LECOUFFE

Software Engineer

DONA SARKAR

USA ✶ BORN 1980

ON WEDNESDAY, Dona built a spaceship to fly to Neptune. On Saturday, she attended school on Mars with a three-headed teacher. After class, Dona and her friends rushed off on a mission to save Earth from a marauding clan of space worms.

Dona and her friends played for hours in her imaginary worlds. No one realized, not even Dona, that she was making up stories because she couldn't read them.

Dona was a baby when she came to Detroit from Nepal with her parents. Her family worked hard, teaching her that when things are tough, you persevere.

When reading, Dona would often trip over words or freeze. She certainly couldn't read under pressure. The worst part was that her classmates picked it up so easily. She wondered, *Why am I struggling? Are they just working harder?*

Dona created little tricks to hide her difficulties. In her fourth-grade class, the students took turns reading aloud according to where they were sitting. The night before, Dona would take the book home. She counted out the paragraphs to find hers and then practiced "over and over and over again" until she almost had it memorized—anything to avoid hearing, "Wow, Dona's stupid. She can't read."

Dona got by in school, buoyed by decent grades in math and science. Outside the classroom, she was a whirlwind of creativity, sewing her own clothes, writing stories, and even painting her own wallpaper designs. Her friends imagined she'd become a writer or theater director.

In high school, Dona and her father read snippets of newspaper articles together. Many stories celebrated kids who studied computers and then started their own companies.

Dona's father was always her cheerleader. "Look at all these boys doing a computer science degree and starting companies and being CEOs," he said. "If boys can do it, you can do it."

Taking her father's advice, Dona jumped in. But without any coding experience, she failed her first class "really badly. I mean, really badly," she remembers. As she worked at it, code started to make sense. She loved that it would tell her right away if it was right or wrong. "Code either works or it doesn't," says Dona. "It doesn't laugh at you."

Pursuing software development as her primary career, Dona built all sorts of apps and tools. What she loved most was creating tools to teach people—from students through adults changing careers—to build apps without learning to code. "It's tech for everyone, a workshop for the world to play in," Dona remarks.

But Dona's imagination couldn't be contained to one space. She now has an array of side projects, from writing fiction to launching a fashion line, and is constantly tinkering with her next new idea.

In her thirties, Dona learned that she had dyslexia. Suddenly, it hit her: *This is why reading was so much harder for me!* But she also realized that her dyslexia fueled her creativity. "If I hadn't been dyslexic, I don't think I would have had such an amazingly creative life," Dona says. "I would have relied on reading other people's words and not creating my own."

“It’s not an *or*, it’s an *and*. My *ands* have led to all sorts of extraordinary things.”

DONA SARKAR

ILLUSTRATION BY PAOLA ROLLO

Director

STEVEN SPIELBERG

USA ✶ BORN DECEMBER 18, 1946

AS NIGHT FELL, the tree outside Steven's window transformed into a monster casting tentacled shadows across his bedroom. Steven shrank under his covers as the monster's fingers inched closer. Across the room, the crack in his wall popped open. The tiny eyes of the wall creatures peered out. Seeing the young boy in peril, the creatures leaped into action and defeated the dark monster. Steven would live another day.

Steven had a vivid imagination. It would often get the best of him, making the smallest things terrifying! He learned to mold his fears into adventures, finding that "the stories always vanquish the fear."

Although doted on at home, Steven remembers himself as an awkward child—"the weird, skinny kid with acne"—who often felt like an outsider. Two years behind his class in reading, he dreaded having to read out loud. He knew he would stumble over the words and feel embarrassed.

He didn't know he had dyslexia. Nobody did. Steven's teachers assumed he wasn't working hard enough, and his parents didn't understand why their bright, creative son brought home such low grades.

Steven's imagination found an outlet, though, when he was twelve. He borrowed his father's 8mm camera to make a film. The short Western, *The Last Gunfight*, earned him his Boy Scout photography badge and ignited a passion.

From then on, after school "I would not go to friends' houses to play. I would go to my bedroom, and I would sit with my little editing machine," Steven remembers.

At sixteen, he made a full-length feature called *Firelight*. His father rented a local movie theater, and his family, friends, and neighbors flocked to see it.

Determined to make his way into the movie business, Steven applied to film school. The University of Southern California rejected him. Twice. But he wouldn't give up. *I'm going to do this, or I'm going to die trying,* he thought. At last, he was admitted to California State College (now University), Long Beach in 1965 and went on to an internship at Universal Studios.

There, in 1968, he had the opportunity to make a short film for a handful of theaters. Steven created *Amblin*, a love story about two hippies hitchhiking across a desert. The film won awards at both the Venice and Atlanta film festivals. Universal was so impressed that they offered him a contract, making him the youngest director ever to sign with a major studio.

Steven had a knack for making people feel like his stories were real. His movie *Jaws*, about a terrifying shark, was so captivating that people stopped going to the beach after seeing it. It was a blockbuster hit, and Steven became a star at age twenty-nine. He went on to make over fifty films, becoming one of the most popular and innovative directors in film history.

At sixty years old, while learning about his son's dyslexia, Steven finally discovered that he was dyslexic too. While he wishes he had known earlier, he has learned to adjust. It might take him three times longer to read something than it does other people, but he doesn't let that bother him. "I'm committed to never feeling ashamed of myself," Steven says. "All those horrible, traumatic years I spent as a kid became what I draw from creatively today."

"You can dart between raindrops to get where you need to go. [Dyslexia] won't hold you back."

STEVEN SPIELBERG

ILLUSTRATION BY MY TIEN PHAM

Writer & Professor

OCEAN VUONG

USA ✶ BORN 1988

OCEAN SAT IN THE LIBRARY during recess, listening to cassette tapes. He was avoiding the boys outside who picked on him for his small size and soft voice. Ocean felt like he didn't belong.

Named for the body of water stretching between Vietnam and America, Ocean was from two worlds but not at home in either. He'd lived in America since he was a toddler and didn't remember Vietnam. But at home, he listened to his grandmother's stories from Vietnam, spoke Vietnamese, and ate Vietnamese food. He felt in between.

At school, Ocean bounced between his regular classroom and English as a Second Language class. He was behind in reading and writing. But being pulled out of class for extra help felt like another signal he was different.

Reading time was particularly stressful. While his classmates bounded through books, Ocean slowly picked his way along, needing to pay close attention to each part of a word to get it right.

Desperate to blend in, he became a master imitator. "I couldn't read, so I would pick up a book based on the cover, like *Goosebumps*. I would wait until the kid in front of me turned the page. Then I would turn the page. I would camouflage myself," he remembers.

One day, his fourth-grade teacher assigned the class a poem to write. Ocean spent hours with a dictionary finding the perfect words. When he finished "If a Boy Could Dream," a poem about spring and hope, he turned it in proudly.

The next day, his teacher accused him of plagiarism. "Show me the poem you copied," he demanded, waving Ocean's paper in the air. He emptied Ocean's desk onto the floor, searching for the poem he thought Ocean was hiding.

Ocean felt terrified and ashamed. But he also felt a tiny bit powerful. *Oh my goodness,* he thought. *I made an adult, who never looked at me before, get flustered over my words.*

Ocean didn't write again for a long time. But as a teenager, he longed to feel noticed again the way he did that day in fourth grade. He began reading and writing once more, and he decided he wanted to be a poet. It seemed impossible; hardly anyone in his family could even read.

With no path to follow, Ocean attended community college and worked in a café while debating what to do next. Eventually, he found his way to Brooklyn College. There, studying literature and writing and sharing his poems, he finally felt "seen for the first time," he says. Ocean realized that needing to look at words carefully, to examine each part, ultimately made him a better writer. His dyslexia was not an obstacle but a strength. Still, a life of writing seemed like a fairy tale.

That changed with Professor Ben Lerner. A passionate teacher and accomplished writer, he helped Ocean map out a path. "He convinced me I could be a professional writer," Ocean remembers.

Ocean became a professor of creative writing at the University of Massachusetts. He has authored several books and poetry collections and won many awards, like the Whiting Award for Poetry and the MacArthur Genius Grant. Yet he still sees a finished piece of writing as a tiny miracle, never to be expected or taken for granted.

"Everything worthwhile is hard to do."

OCEAN VUONG

ILLUSTRATION BY PAOLA ROLLO

Entrepreneur

CLIFF WEITZMAN

ISRAEL + USA ✶ BORN 1990

CLIFF WEITZMAN was a model first-grade student. He studiously ran his finger under lines of text in class, put in hours at the library, and walked around everywhere with a book under his arm.

But Cliff had a secret: He couldn't read. "I knew the rules, every rule," he says. "But when I applied [them], it just did. Not. Work." He knew the rules so well that he even taught his younger sister how to read.

He desperately wanted to learn. "Carrying around that book, I imagined that, one day, I'd be able to read it," says Cliff. "And the book I wanted to read the most was *Harry Potter.*" Cliff would settle himself in the library after school with *Harry Potter and the Sorcerer's Stone* open before him—only to wake forty minutes later with the librarian hovering over him and a little puddle of drool where his head rested on page three. Reading was exhausting.

When Cliff found out he was dyslexic, he was in third grade. He thought, *Finally! I'm not broken, I'm not dumb, and I am definitely not lazy! Now that I know the problem, I can fix it.*

Cliff's father started reading *Harry Potter* to him every night before bed. Cliff loved it. When he got his hands on a *Harry Potter* audiobook, he listened to it twenty-two times in a row, memorizing the whole first chapter.

Harry Potter was just the beginning of learning through listening. "I could learn everything—from how people in other countries live through history to how to code," Cliff says. He was always listening—while biking to school, doing chores, running errands. Soon, Cliff was listening to two books a week.

He particularly loved stories about people working through challenges: explorers, inventors, entrepreneurs, scientists. "Stories make everything seem achievable, and every obstacle overcome-able," Cliff notes.

Cliff stopped trying to learn like other kids and started asking for permission to do things differently, like having questions read to him and getting extra time for his schoolwork.

In college, most textbooks weren't available as audiobooks. Undeterred, Cliff watched some videos and hacked together a system on his computer to convert photos of the pages into audio. "There is no way that I could take the classes I was taking if I didn't have audiobooks," he says.

Cliff didn't stop with the audiobook converter. He loved to invent things, and his enthusiasm inspired others to join in. He and his friends built products ranging from a skateboard brake to a payments app to a solar cell. He was interested in so many things, he found it hard to commit to any one of his creations.

Finally, by the time he was graduating, Cliff discovered what he wanted to make. It had been right in front of him the whole time. In 2016, he created a simple app to turn any text into an instant audiobook. Now every day, millions of people rely on his company, Speechify, to read and learn.

Running a startup isn't easy, but he's been training for this. "I have an unfair advantage," he says, crediting his dyslexia. "From a very young age, I had to figure out how to do the things I wanted even though the initial path was broken. I learned to take risks, to recover from failure, to persevere."

"Anything you want to learn, you can learn. It's simply a matter of, How do you learn?"

CLIFF WEITZMAN

ILLUSTRATION BY CRISTINA PORTOLANO

Football Coach

JOE WHITT JR.

USA ✶ BORN 1978

"GO LONG!" Joe's father called as Joe sprinted across the yard. Glancing back, Joe caught the ball as he ran into an imaginary end zone. Touchdown!

When Joe wasn't playing football, he was talking football—at the dinner table, on the drive to church, even at bedtime.

Joe's dad was a football coach for the town's beloved Auburn Tigers. Young Joe tagged along on recruiting trips, learning how to spot a great player. When he could write plus and minus signs, Joe helped his dad grade game film. Paper and pencil in hand, he watched each play, awarding plus signs for great performances and minuses for mistakes.

Joe shared something else with his dad: dyslexia. In kindergarten, he began visiting Ms. Wingo, the reading teacher. With extra help and hard work, he learned to read.

Yet his difficulties didn't entirely disappear. Joe dreaded the words, "Open your textbooks. Let's start by reading aloud." While his classmates took their turns, Joe frantically tried to memorize his section. He hoped that by the time his turn arrived, the words would come out smoothly. They usually did not.

In those moments, he wondered, *Why can't I be like everyone else?*

Amid his frustration and embarrassment, his father reminded him he was strong, he was smart, and his hard work would lead to success. "Quitters never win," his dad would tell his players, encouraging them to persevere.

Joe would not quit, but he was finished with being embarrassed. In ninth grade, he told all his teachers, "I'm going to do the work, I'm going to make good grades, but I'm not going to read in class, so please, just skip over me." Some teachers were skeptical. Was this kid just trying to get out of work? But by focusing on his people skills, public speaking, and ability to memorize, Joe did well and won his teachers over.

Joe didn't just get by, he became a leader—on the field as a star football player and off the field as class president, athletics president, and school president.

In 1997, Joe joined his father at Auburn University, earning a spot on the team as a wide receiver. After only a few games, however, his injuries began to pile up. Soon it was clear: Joe's football dreams were dead.

Joe was out of the game, but he wasn't leaving the field. He traded in his helmet for a clipboard and got to work as a student coaching assistant.

Coaching used all Joe's gifts, and he'd literally been studying for this since childhood. His new career launched like a rocket, landing him in the NFL as a defensive coach at just twenty-eight.

Joe was tough and demanding, like his dad. But what made Joe an exceptional coach was his ability to teach. He understood that everyone learns differently and adjusted his style for each player. In the off-season, Joe shadowed teachers, learning how the best ones worked with all sorts of students. It paid off. Joe's players became some of the best in the NFL.

Despite the challenges he faced when he was young, Joe sees the positives now. "I didn't want to be dyslexic when I was ten years old," Joe says, "but good things came from it." Being "different" made Joe exceptional.

"Everyone needs help and it's really brave to accept it when it's offered and even braver to ask for help when you need it."

JOE WHITT JR.

ILLUSTRATION BY QUINTON WINTER

Activist

JOSHUA WONG

HONG KONG ✶ BORN 1996

GROWING UP IN HONG KONG, Joshua Wong was a regular kid. He played video games, watched anime, and went to church with his parents on Sunday. "I was a scrawny, nerdy Hong Kong schoolboy," he recalls.

Even as a little boy, Joshua asked lots of questions. In church, while other children were silent, Joshua spoke up. "If God is so full of mercy and kindness, why does he let poor people suffer? We make donations every month; where does that money go?" It was strange for a child to ask such big questions. But he got away with it because adults thought it was cute.

While he was good at talking and asking questions, Joshua struggled with reading and writing. "Simple characters that preschoolers learned in a matter of days, like 'large' (大) and 'very' (太), looked indistinguishable to me," he says.

He knew it wouldn't be easy to get into high school. "I put away my video games and manga and put in over twenty hours of tutoring every week," Joshua says. Going to tutoring was like having a part-time job! But it was worth it: He managed to lift his grades just enough to get into his first-choice high school.

Hong Kong was a beautiful place to grow up, with its towering sky-scrapers and green mountain peaks rising out of the smooth South China Sea. Joshua loved the bustling markets and shopping malls. For 150 years, the United Kingdom governed Hong Kong. When Joshua was a baby, in 1997, Hong Kong returned to China's communist rule. Nervous Hong Kongers wondered what would change for them.

In 2011, when Joshua was in high school, the communist government announced a new school curriculum, National Education, designed to teach only the ideas that China approved. Joshua and his friends agreed: *This is brainwashing! We must do something.*

What could students do against a whole government? And what would the government do if they began to speak up? The adults might not think Joshua was so cute now.

Together with two of his friends, Agnes and Ivan, Joshua started a group called Scholarism and began to fight—on social media, on TV, and on the street, handing out flyers. Soon the cause filled all of Joshua's free time. He felt like a superhero, going to class during the day and rushing out to fight the government after school.

For eighteen months, Joshua talked. More and more people heard his words and joined him. In 2012, after nine days of camping out in front of government headquarters, Joshua led a protest of over a hundred thousand people demanding that the government cancel the National Education program. And the government relented! Joshua, Agnes, Ivan, and the people had won!

But Joshua did not stop there. As China persists in taking Hong Kongers' freedoms away, he continues to speak up. Already imprisoned three times, Joshua lives under constant threat of arrest. But he's far from done. "No matter what happens," Joshua says, "I love Hong Kong, and I will continue my commitment until the day we see a brighter future."

Dyslexia forced Joshua to lean on his voice, and Joshua's words began a movement. The nerdy Hong Kong schoolboy has shown just how powerful a voice can be.

"Even one person can make a difference, no matter the odds. Whatever your age, wherever you are, you can be a part of something far greater than yourself."

JOSHUA WONG

Perspectives

How are YOU brilliant?

Understanding how people are feeling even if they don't tell me. — **SOPHIA, 13**

I'm good at teamwork. — **ROWAN, 9**

I'm good at gymnastics, and I always try my hardest. — **POPPY, 8**

Something I really love is sewing and fashion. I want to be a fashionista when I grow up. — **LOGAN, 11**

Visualizing and sharing my ideas. When I speak about things I'm passionate about, people take it to heart and listen. — **CAMERON, 15**

Basketball. Cycling. Scooting. — **BARNEY, 15**

Expressing myself through art instead of words. I see in pictures. If I can visualize it, then I can create it—drawings, costumes, dresses, pottery, cakes.
— **GIANNA, 16**

I'm a super problem solver. I can picture complex systems in my head, and I love to talk!
— **ZACHARY, 8**

Coming up with creative ways to solve problems, especially building things. I love to build robots and mechanics. I also love chatting and making friends. — **GRAYSON, 10**

Perseverance is one of my biggest things. It's hard but it's so worth it. — **KAITLIN, 21**

Acting and singing. I do musicals and play productions.
— **ZAHRAH, 12**

I'm brilliant in my heart. — **MILLIE, 8**

What advice would you give to others with dyslexia?

School can be difficult and frustrating, but it will get better and you will be amazing! — **ZACHARY, 8**

Advocate for yourself and own it. Go out there and be proud.
— **ZAHRAH, 12**

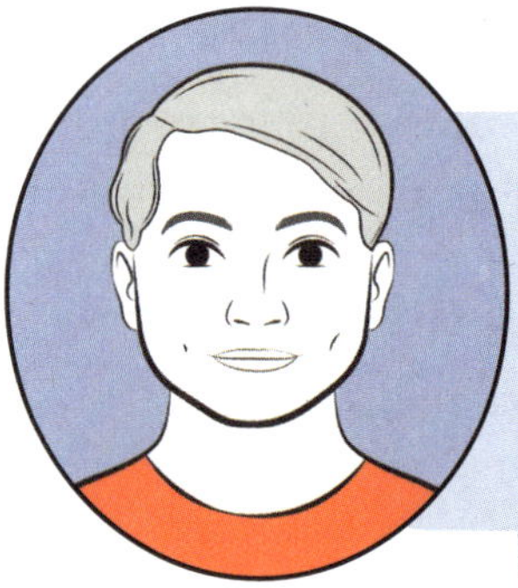

Don't give up trying. You can learn, just in a different way. — **ROWAN, 9**

With letters and words, it takes longer. Take your time. — **MILLIE, 8**

Be confident in yourself, believe in yourself, and just keep reminding yourself that you can do it. — **LOGAN, 11**

Find what works for you. For me, it's visualization . . . diagrams and drawing things out. — **CAMERON, 15**

Don't be so hard on yourself . . . It gets better over time. Always try to find the positive parts, like having different ideas and perspectives.

— **GIANNA, 16**

Everyone has their own experience with dyslexia. Ask for help. If you don't, it can become a big weight to carry.

— **AYANA, 14**

Know that there are many different kinds and ways that people are smart, like academic smart, people smart, body smart, music smart, art smart, creative smart. — **SOPHIA, 13**

Work hard and ask questions . . . don't be too shy to ask.

— **BARNEY, 15**

You've got to be brave and give things a go, even if you're not as good at first. — **BEN, 10**

What do you wish everyone knew about dyslexia?

It's just a different way of thinking. — **BARNEY, 15**

Dyslexia is like a fish in a tree only if the fish doesn't give up it will grow wings and soar among the stars. — **FOX, 18**

There are amazing people who have dyslexia. We are just as capable, but we need different things to be just as successful.
— **KAITLIN, 21**

That it is not a disability, but it is a superpower. Find your superpower!
— **BENJAMIN, 11**

It allows you to think outside the box and be creative. I wish people knew that. — **AYANA, 14**

Be patient. A kid with dyslexia might not do something as quickly. It might take us a little more time.

— **LOGAN, 11**

Dyslexia might even make you smarter because we have to focus more. When you focus more, not only do you get better at it, but you understand it more. And you might even become a better reader and writer because of it.

— **GRAYSON, 10**

We are very intelligent. We just have to be more flexible with our learning processes.

— **SOPHIA, 13**

I wish people knew what goes on in our brains and how amazing we are! — **ZACHARY, 8**

Experts

What do you wish everyone knew about dyslexia?

Dyslexia is broad; it's not just about reading and writing. It's so much more. It's a fundamental difference in the way our brains are structured. It's not a weakness, not a strength. It's a difference, and differences come with different strengths and weaknesses.

— **NATALIE BROOKS, FOUNDER OF DYSLEXIA IN ADULTS**

Children learn differently. Many children need to learn in creative ways—visually, nonlinearly, multisensory. The current education system wasn't created with neurodiverse thinkers in mind. Assessments don't reveal a child's advantages and true potential. — **MARCIA BRISSETT-BAILEY BSC PG DIP MA, TRUSTEE OF WALTHAM FOREST DYSLEXIA ASSOCIATION**

The teaching approaches that help dyslexic students are beneficial to all students. — **SUE GONZALES, LITERACY SPECIALIST**

That a dyslexic mind isn't simply trying but failing to be a "normal" mind, but is instead patterned in ways that create advantages in some functions and disadvantages in others. The disadvantages occur in functions like decoding and spelling, but the advantages include things like three-dimensional spatial reasoning ability, seeing connections between ideas and concepts, memory for experience, problem solving by insight, and making predictions. These strengths, rather than difficulties, are the true "heart and soul" of the dyslexic mind and the reason why as many as one in five individuals are dyslexic. Dyslexic minds are a large part of the human family because they contribute important strengths that make our societies more creative, resilient, and adaptive, and coming to recognize and nurture these strengths—and the dyslexic individuals who possess them—will benefit us all. — **DRS. BROCK AND FERNETTE EIDE, AUTHORS OF *THE DYSLEXIC ADVANTAGE***

Dyslexia Basics

HOW THE BRAIN WORKS

Think of the brain as a team

The different parts of the brain are like different players on the team. They play different positions with different jobs, but they all need to work together. Depending on what we're doing, some players will be asked to take the lead while others can take a break.

All day, in everything they do, the players communicate with each other and do their specific jobs.

Some tasks are more difficult than others

The more players a task requires, the more complex it is. Simple tasks feel easy. The team seems to naturally play their parts and get the job done. Other tasks, like riding a bike or doing a math problem, require specific training and practice to learn.

Every team is different

No brain is the best at everything, just like no one team is best in every sport. We all have some players that are stronger at different roles than others and players who work together really well. When activities involve our strongest players, they feel easy.

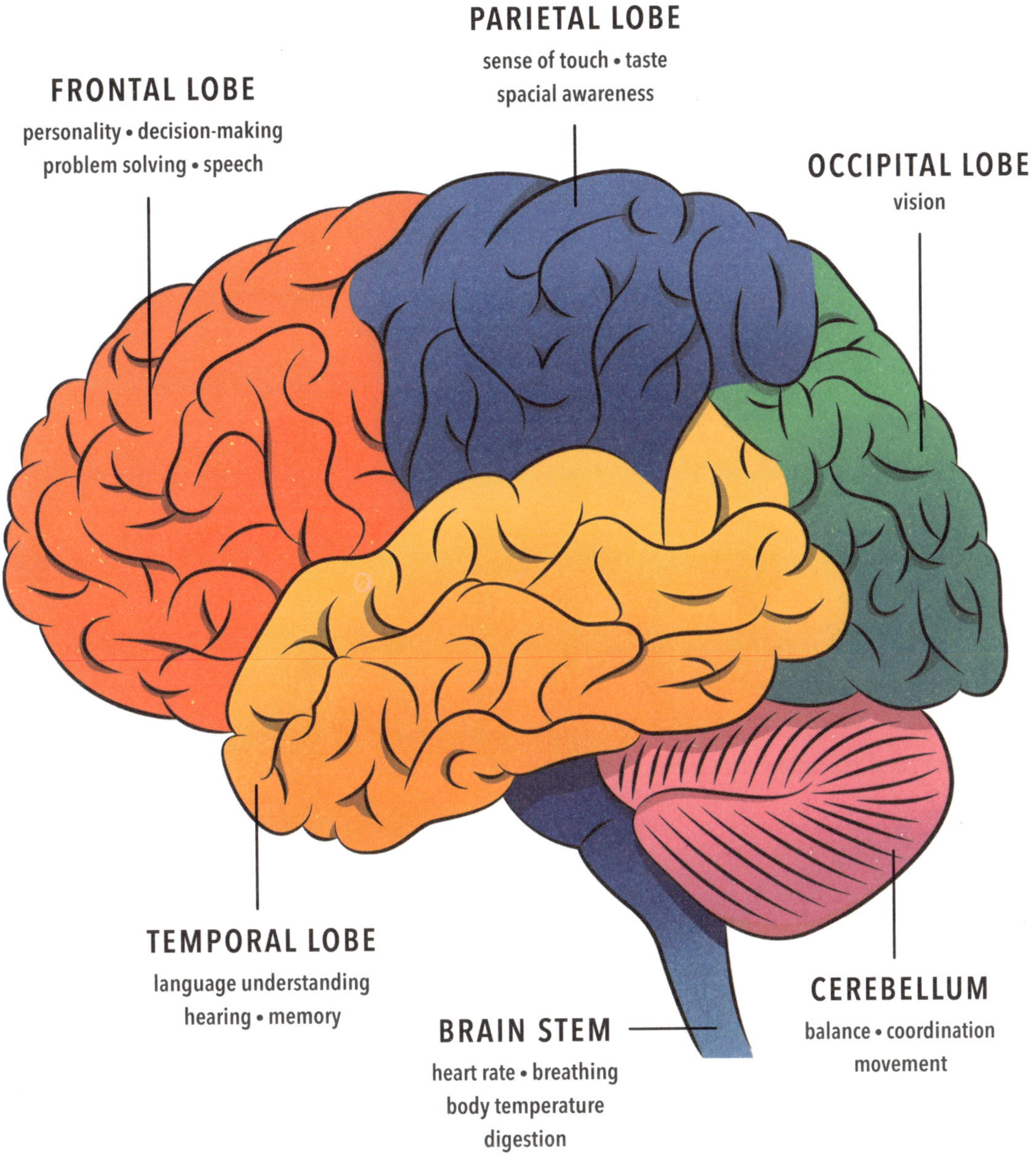
PARIETAL LOBE
sense of touch • taste
spacial awareness
FRONTAL LOBE
personality • decision-making
problem solving • speech
OCCIPITAL LOBE
vision
TEMPORAL LOBE
language understanding
hearing • memory
BRAIN STEM
heart rate • breathing
body temperature
digestion
CEREBELLUM
balance • coordination
movement

READING IS DIFFICULT

Our brains aren't born knowing how to read or even how to learn to read. They need to be trained. When we read, several different parts of the brain need to follow rules and work together as a team. Some teams pick it up quickly while other teams need a lot more practice and coaching.

It's particularly difficult for the dyslexic brain

In the dyslexic brain, the players who need to work together for reading and writing don't communicate well, and they might trip up on such tasks as breaking down sounds or connecting symbols to words. At the same time, the players in charge of understanding and articulating language may be very strong.

Dyslexic brains need specific training that focuses on each skill that's part of reading. It can be a lot of work. However, with the right support, dyslexic learners can learn to read well and even to love doing it.

Our brains can grow and change

Everyone has things that feel easy and things that feel hard. When we work on something that is hard (but not too hard), our brain gets stronger. The different players improve, and the connections between the players increase. Over time, the hard thing feels easier.

Strengths step up to balance weaknesses

When a task is hard or when one player struggles, the stronger players step up to help the team succeed. Although dyslexic minds may struggle with reading and writing, they also have patterns of strength that may lead to advantage in other areas such as problem solving and creativity.

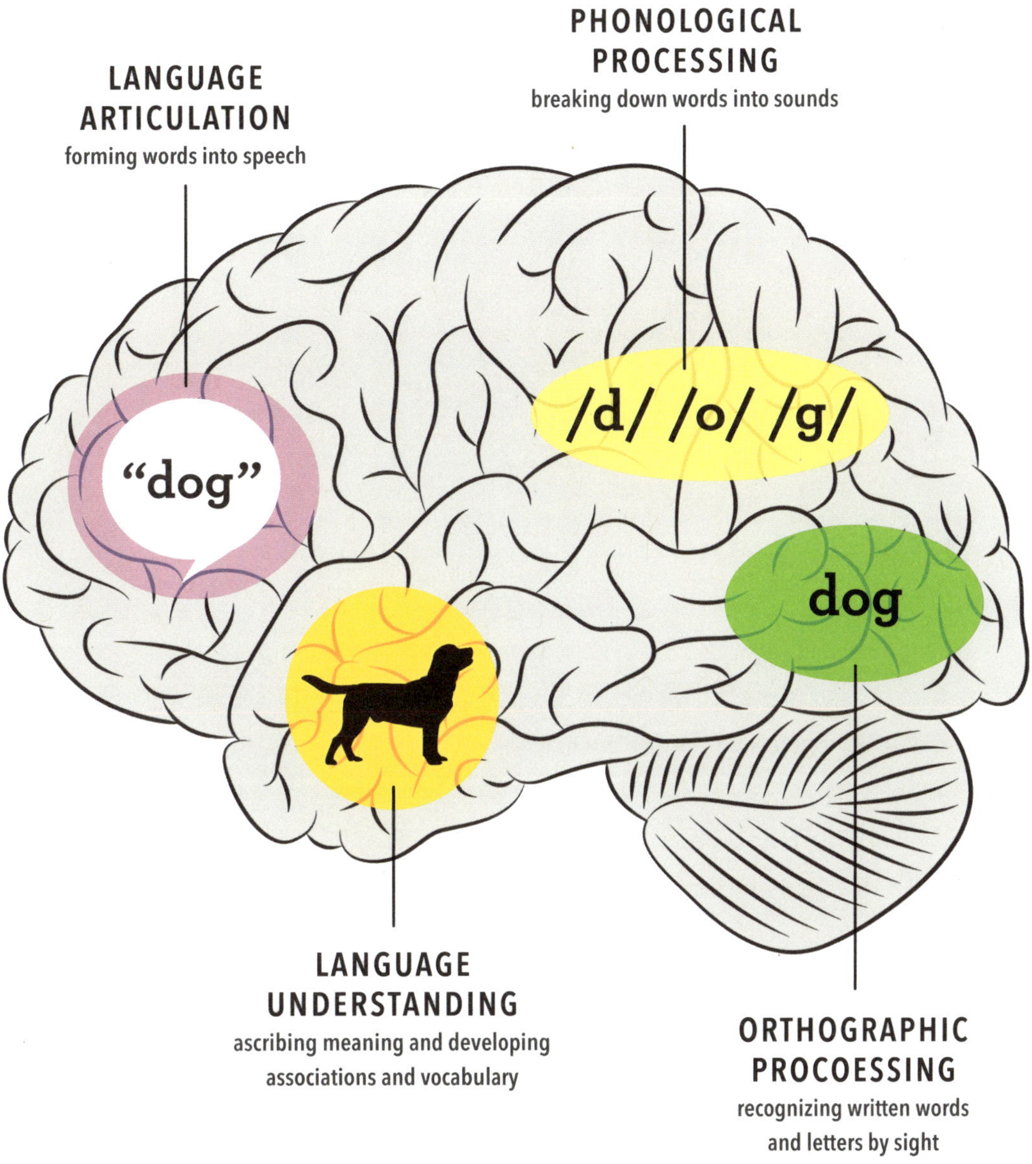

Informed by the work of neuroscientist Dr. Fumiko Hoeft, MD, PhD,
Professor of Child & Adolescent Psychiatry, Director of BrainLENS at UCSF,
Director of the Brain Imaging Research Center at UConn, and Deputy Director of UCSF Dyslexia Center

WHAT IS DYSLEXIA ANYWAY?

Dyslexia is a learning difference. It's a general term covering difficulty in learning to read or interpret words, letters, and other symbols. However, dyslexia doesn't affect intelligence. It's simply a difference in how the brain processes information.

IS . . .

Common. Approximately 15–20% of people have symptoms of dyslexia. It's the number one cause of illiteracy and school dropout.

On a continuum. Dyslexia varies in severity and with the specific types of strengths and challenges people experience.

Something that runs in families. Dyslexia has a genetic component. If a parent has dyslexia, their children may also.

Possible to identify as early as preschool. Screening for the risk factors of dyslexia in young children helps identify risk so that they can receive support before they struggle.

Lifelong. Dyslexia isn't something that is "cured." However, the impact and experience can change at different stages in a person's life. Dyslexic learners can become highly successful students and adults.

ISN'T . . .

Reflective of intelligence or potential. Dyslexia occurs in people of all backgrounds and intellectual levels. Dyslexic learners can be very bright or even gifted.

Temporary. It's not something that's grown out of. However, the worst of the challenges tend to be experienced in early education. With support and appropriate teaching methods, the challenges can be overcome.

A visual problem. It's a neurological difference. Dyslexics "see" the same thing as everyone else, but dyslexic brains process the information differently.

The same for everyone. While dyslexic learners share some common difficulties, each person has a diverse set of challenges and strengths.

Only negative. The brain differences cause specific struggles with language but also advantages in other areas like creativity and problem solving.

COMMON MYTHS & MISCONCEPTIONS

Misconception	Reality
Helping a child with dyslexia is only about remediating weaknesses.	Remediation in areas of weakness is necessary. However, for a child to thrive, identifying and playing to strengths is critical.
Dyslexic learners won't ever read well or love reading.	With the right teaching, dyslexic learners can learn to read well. While they may read relatively slowly, many grow to love reading and writing.
Everyone with dyslexia feels the same way about it. Kids should feel positive about it and see it as a gift or "superpower."	Since children primarily experience the challenges of dyslexia, many do not see it positively. That can change over time. Depending on their experiences, adults think of their dyslexia as a disability, a difference, or a "superpower."
Dyslexia affects more boys than girls.	Males are diagnosed with dyslexia more frequently than females, but it affects genders equally.

Misconception	Reality
All children will learn to read eventually if given the time.	Children with dyslexia require explicit, structured reading instruction. The earlier they receive this, the faster they will make progress. In fact, the structured literacy approaches that dyslexic learners need benefit all children.
Reading is a natural process.	Reading was invented by humans. It is a complex process requiring multiple parts of the brain to work together. Learning to read requires training.
Dyslexia only affects reading and writing.	Dyslexia can affect memory, organization, timekeeping, multitasking, and communication.
People with dyslexia can only do certain jobs.	Dyslexia does not determine career path. While there are some common paths, like entrepreneurship and creative fields, a person with dyslexia can pursue any field.

Appendix

BRILLIANT HALL OF FAME

Let's hear it for the early believers in *Brilliantly Dyslexic* and, more importantly, believers that thinking differently can be amazing and that the world is more beautiful for it. You are brilliant!

MAX AND NATE BEACHAM

ISABEL MILLIE BLACKBURN

RYE LAURO CUSTODIO

ERIN DEMICCO

SUE GONZALES

KRISTEN GUNDLACH

LILY HANNAN

SALLY KIM

CLAIRE KING

HEATH WESLEY LINAM

ABBIE LLOYD

ALYSSA MOSES

KAREN OLSON

KATE PIPER

KRISTIN SIMONS

EMILY STARFAS

JESSA THOMAS

NICKI WINTER

MIMI ZORA

AND YOU!

ILLUSTRATORS

Illustrators are listed in order of first appearance in the book.

GILLIAN DREHER • Maggie Aderin-Pocock, Beryl Benacerraf

GERALDINE SY • Ann Bancroft, Richard Branson, Perspectives and Dyslexia Basics illustrations

PAUL TRUDEAU • Ruqsana Begum

MONICA GARWOOD • Darcey Bussell, Elisabeth Prueitt

ANNIE GALVIN • Heather Day

MERCEDES DEBELLARD • Kate Evans

CHRIS KING • Vernon François

HSIAO-RON CHENG • John Hoke

LI ZHANG • David Hornik

LIAM BRAZIER • Earvin "Magic" Johnson

JUSTINE LECOUFFE • Carol Moseley Braun, Dona Sarkar

DÉBORA ISLAS • Maria Naggaga

MARTA SIGNORI • Byron Pitts

PAOLA ROLLO • Steven Spielberg, Cliff Weitzman

MY TIEN PHAM • Ocean Vuong

CRISTINA PORTOLANO • Joe Whitt Jr.

QUINTON WINTER • Joshua Wong

ACKNOWLEDGMENTS

Thank you to our *Brilliantly Dyslexic* community on Kickstarter. You believed in this book before you could hold it. We are forever grateful.

Thank you to the people featured in the book for sharing your stories with the world. Some of you shared your story in detail for the first time. Thank you for trusting me with it. I hope I did it justice.

Thank you to the village of people who brought this book to life. To all the advisors, test families, teachers, and experts for sharing feedback and believing in what this project could become. Without your encouragement, I wouldn't have had the courage to create it. To the team of collaborators: Kristine Brogno, whose design talents made it beautiful; S. Robin Larin, whose critique and editing polished each story; Becky Noelle, whose proofreading cared for every detail; and every illustrator who contributed their talents.

Thank you to my mother, Anne, for reading through each story and helping me find its heart. Without you, this book would not exist.

Thank you to Paul, for believing in the vision, for living every triumph and every disappointment with me, and for always supporting this project despite the immense time and resources it has required.

A NOTE FROM THE CREATORS

This book was created by a mom and daughter. Liz is the author, and Quinn, with her keen eye for all things visual, is the creative director.

From Liz...

We created *Brilliantly Dyslexic* because we needed this book. Like many dyslexic learners, Quinn was having a hard time at school. Comparing herself to her classmates, she felt like she didn't measure up. When I started telling her about some incredible people with dyslexia, she lit up. She was surprised. How could it be that someone could be both dyslexic and smart? The more I shared with her, the more her perspective seemed to shift. Perhaps her difficulties weren't meant to be her whole story after all.

While there is a lot of information online about amazing people with dyslexia, we couldn't find something designed for children. So, I started writing, filling a binder with stories.

Seeing the impact these stories had on my daughter, I began to wonder: What if this situation isn't unique for us? What if we made this a book for the many children who are looking for stories that they can find themselves in?

After two years of writing, editing, and working with illustrators, we're thrilled that this book is in your hands.

From Quinn...

I hope that this book helps kids and teachers understand that when you're dyslexic, you think differently. Sometimes it makes things harder in school, but it's not better or worse. We're just as smart as other people.

One of my strengths is that I see things that other people don't notice, like with the art and design for the book. As the creative director, I've picked artists, helped design the cover, and given feedback on sketches and final approval on the illustrations. I love that all the different art makes each story feel different, just like each person is different.

ABOUT THE RESEARCH

We have done our best to be thorough in our research, immersing ourselves in books, interviews, articles, and podcasts. Whenever possible, we consulted the subjects themselves, interviewing the people featured and sharing stories for edits. We learned more about these incredible people than could possibly be included. Each story is merely a glimpse into their lives.

We've made every effort to present true, well-researched stories. For more information about our sources, visit www.brilliantlydyslexic.com

SIGNS OF DYSLEXIA

Dyslexia looks different in different people. However, there are common signs and indicators. Each child may exhibit a different combination. One may exhibit a few signs profoundly while another will exhibit many moderately.

Primary indicators for school-age children

- has difficulty spelling
- has/had difficulty learning letter names and the sounds they make
- has/had difficulty reading words
- reads below grade level
- requires extra help in school because of problems in reading and spelling

Note: This list is not a replacement for formal screening or assessment.

It's not just about reading, writing, and spelling. Dyslexia can make other things tricky, things like . . .

- remembering names
- following multistep instructions
- telling time
- remembering the alphabet, days of the week, or months
- identifying left vs. right
- getting and staying organized
- remembering the words for things

Dyslexia can show up alone or with some "friends." The following are a few common learning differences that can overlap with dyslexia.

Dyscalculia: Difficulty with math and working with numbers. It isn't as well studied as dyslexia, but some experts believe that it is quite common.

Dysgraphia: Difficulty with writing, specifically the skills required to produce writing such as forming letters, handwriting, and typing.

ADHD: Difficulty with focus, hyperactivity, and/or impulsivity. It can show up in different ways for different people. While focus is generally a challenge, people with ADHD can hyperfocus on activities that they find interesting.

HELPFUL WEBSITES

International Dyslexia Association – dyslexiaida.org
Fact Sheets about dyslexia, dysgraphia, ADHD. Suggested readings for parents and teachers.

Understood – understood.org
Articles and information about various learning differences.

For more resources for parents, teachers, librarians, and students, visit: www.brilliantlydyslexic.com/resources

www.brilliantlydyslexic.com

Join the *Brilliantly Dyslexic* community . . .
Facebook: www.facebook.com/brilliantlydyslexic
Instagram: @brilliantlydyslexic
Twitter: @dyslexicbook

Love *Brilliantly Dyslexic*? Please take a moment to post a review of the book, wherever you like to review things.

This is the Dyslexia Symbol. Wherever you see it—at a library, on a book, or hanging from a necklace—you'll find a dyslexia friendly space. For more information, visit www.pqbd.org

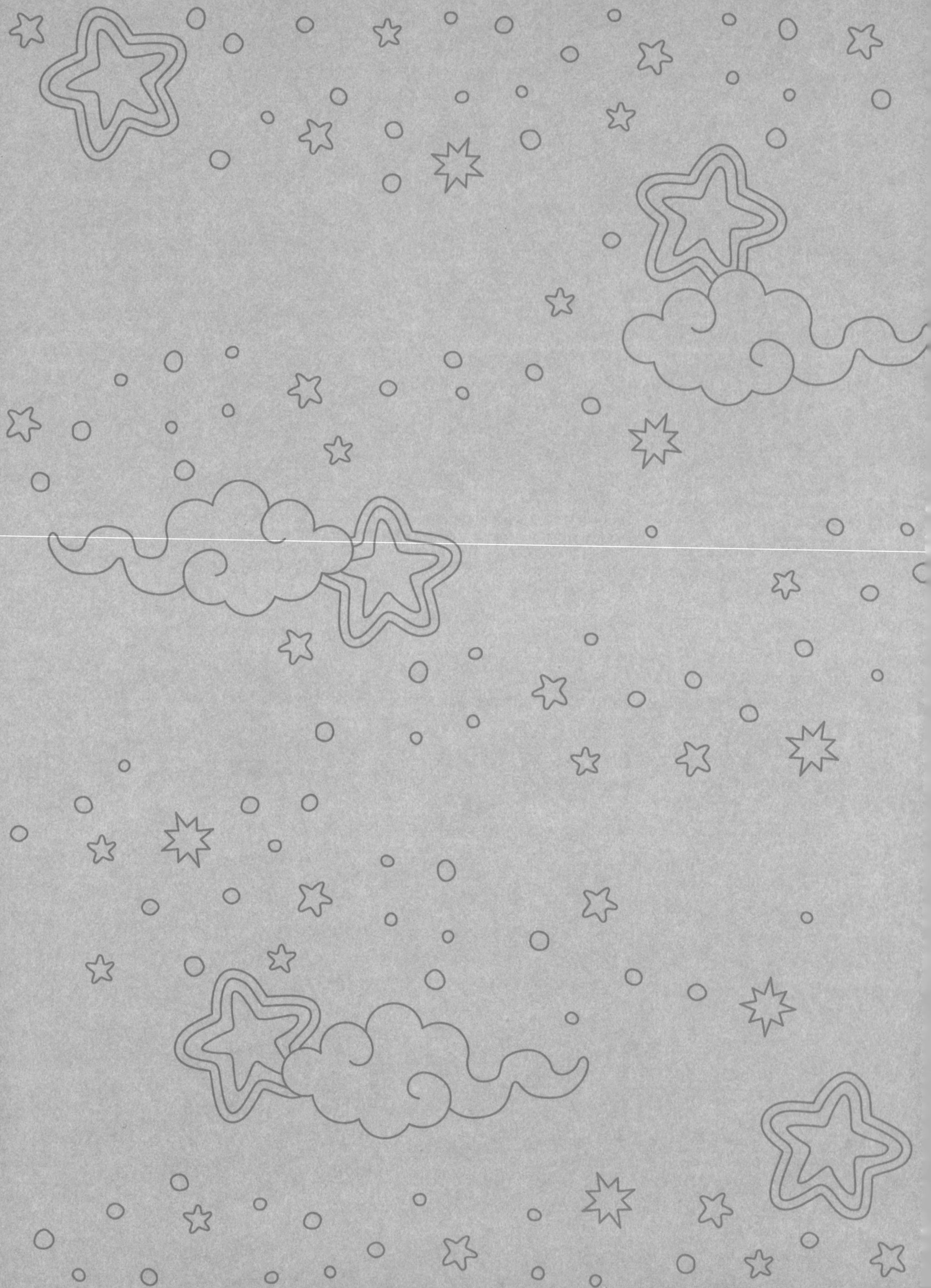